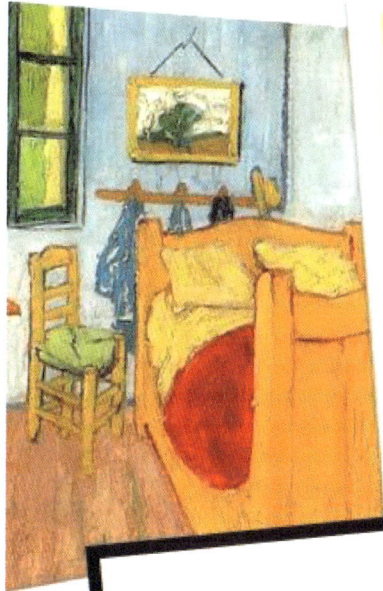

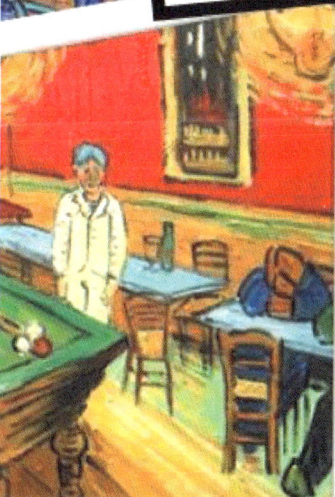
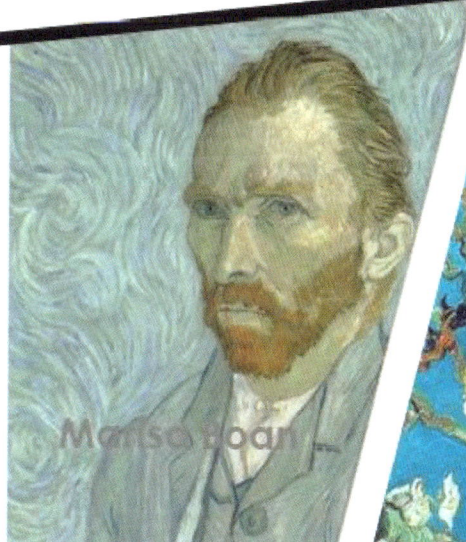

Vincent Van Gogh

Biography & Coloring Book

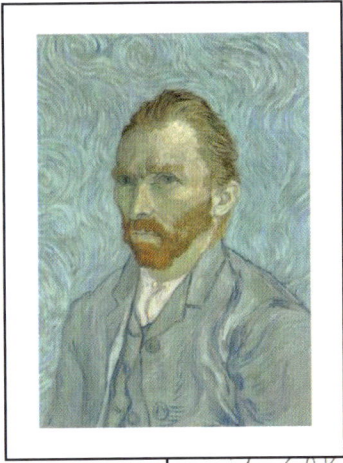

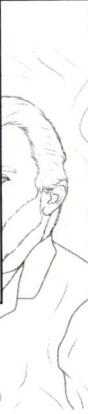

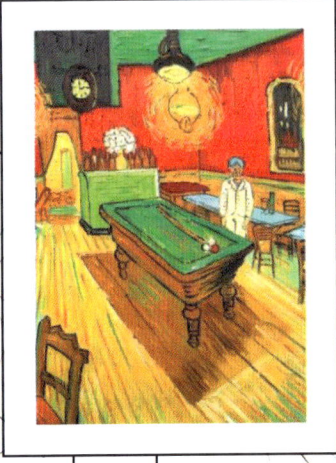

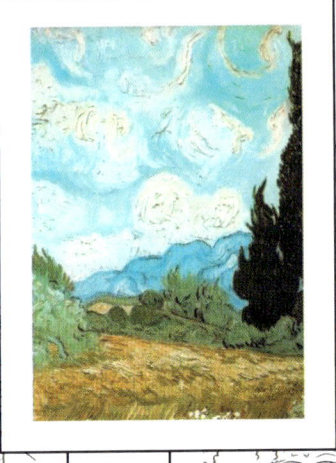

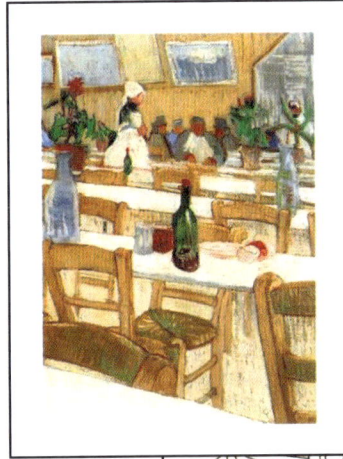

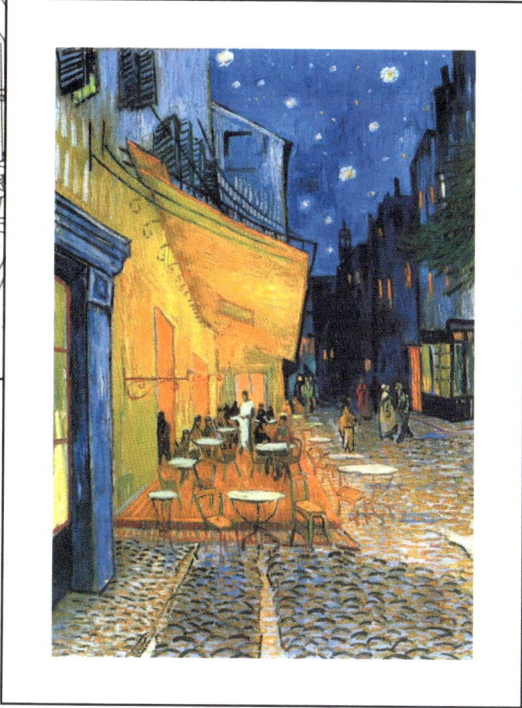

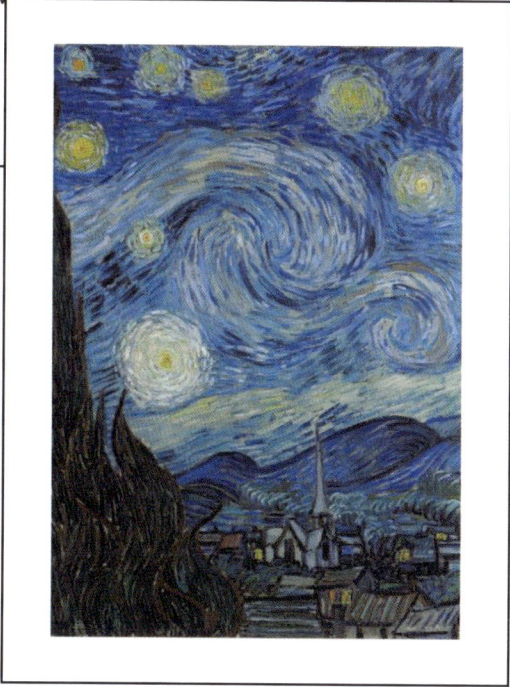

Vincent Van Gogh

Vincent Van Gogh was born on March 30, 1853 in Zundert, Netherlands. His father was a minister. He had two brothers and three sisters. His favorite brother was named Theo.

Vincent had many different jobs before he became an artist. He was a teacher and a minister and worked in a bookstore. He loved to draw as a child and when he was around 27 years old he decided to become an artist.

When he first started drawing and painting he used pencils, charcoal, and oil paints. He liked to use dark colors like black, brown, and green. Many of his drawings and paintings were of people at work. They were very dark pictures so some of them looked sad and dreary.

No one wanted to buy Van Gogh's paintings. He would write letters to his brother, Theo, who lived in Paris and ask him for help. Theo told him about a new style of painting called Impressionism. Vincent decided to move to Paris and try this new style. He started painting scenes of people in the streets and cafes. He also started using bright colored paints.
He loved the brighter colors and the light of the sun.

By 1889, Van Gogh became sick and could not take care of himself. He had to go into a hospital, but he was able to continue painting. He painted every day. He liked to paint trees and paintings with swirling colors. He did not get better while he was in the hospital. He died on July , 29, 1890.

Van Gogh was not famous when he was alive. Now he is one of the most famous artists in the whole world. No one wanted to buy his paintings when he was alive. Now, everyone loves his paintings, and they are worth millions of dollars!

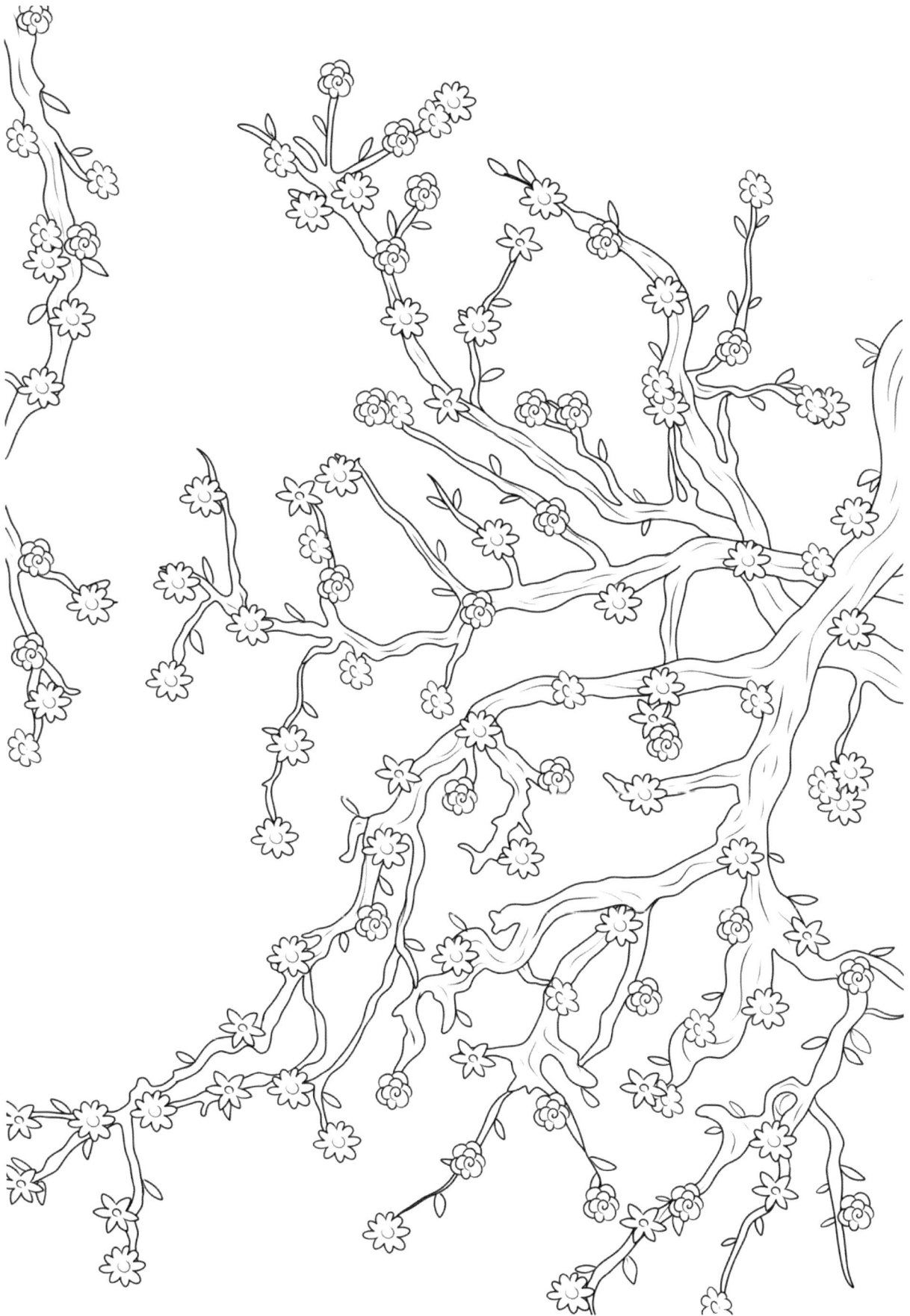

Index of Paintings

Self Portrait
The Night Café
Wheat Field With Cypresses
Interior of a Restaurant
Postman Joseph Roulin
Irises
Bedroom in Arles
Still Life - Vase with Fifteen Sunflowers
Café Terrace at Night
Starry Night
Branches With Almond Blossoms

MAGICSPELLSFORTEACHERS.COM

Available at
amazon

Printed in Great Britain
by Amazon